EXPLORING WORLD CULTURES

Libya

Alicia Z. Klepeis

Cavendish
Square

New York

Published in 2021 by Cavendish Square Publishing, LLC
243 5th Avenue, Suite 136, New York, NY 10016

Website: cavendishsq.com

This publication represents the opinions and views of the author based on his or her personal experience, knowledge, and research. The information in this book serves as a general guide only. The author and publisher have used their best efforts in preparing this book and disclaim liability rising directly or indirectly from the use and application of this book.

All websites were available and accurate when this book was sent to press.

Library of Congress Cataloging-in-Publication Data

Names: Klepeis, Alicia, 1971- author.
Title: Libya / Alicia Z Klepeis.
Description: First edition. | New York : Cavendish Square, 2021. |
Series: Exploring world cultures | Includes bibliographical references and index.
Identifiers: LCCN 2019040732 (print) | LCCN 2019040733 (ebook) |
ISBN 9781502656759 (library binding) | ISBN 9781502656735 (paperback) |
ISBN 9781502656742 (set) | ISBN 9781502656766 (ebook)
Subjects: LCSH: Libya--Juvenile literature.
Classification: LCC DT215 .K55 2021 (print) | LCC DT215 (ebook) |
DDC 961.2--dc23
LC record available at https://lccn.loc.gov/2019040732
LC ebook record available at https://lccn.loc.gov/2019040733

Editor: Kristen Susienka
Copy Editor: Nathan Heidelberger
Designer: Jessica Nevins

The photographs in this book are used by permission and through the courtesy of: Cover Ekaterina Vidyasova/Shutterstock.com; pp. 4, 20, 25 MAHMUD TURKIA/AFP/Getty Images; p. 5 Abdalwahab ali/Shutterstock.com; p. 6 pavalena/Shutterstock.com; p. 7 MrLis/Shutterstock.com; p. 8 John Copland/Shutterstock.com; p. 9 rm/Shutterstock.com; pp. 10, 12 ABDULLAH DOMA/AFP/Getty Images; p. 11 MOHAMMED ABED/AFP/GettyImages; p. 13 © iStockphoto.com/Leeman; p. 14 Zoltan Tarlacz/Shutterstock.com; p. 15 cinoby/E+/Getty Images; p. 16 Charles O. Cecil/Alamy Stock Photo; p. 17 parasola.net/Alamy Stock Photo; p. 18 Noctiluxx/iStock/Getty Images Plus; p. 19 Gim42/iStock/Getty Images Plus; p. 21 TheRunoman/Shutterstock.com; p. 22 UfaBizPhoto/Shutterstock.com; p. 23 tourdottk/Shutterstock.com; p. 24 robertharding/Alamy Stock Photo; p. 26 SALAH HABIBI/AFP/Getty Images; p. 27 In Pictures Ltd./Corbis via Getty Images; p. 28 © iStockphoto.com/hipokrat; p. 29 Ahmed Alkmeshi/Shutterstock.com.

Some of the images in this book illustrate individuals who are models. The depictions do not imply actual situations or events.

CPSIA compliance information: Batch #CS20CSQ: For further information contact Cavendish Square Publishing LLC, New York, New York, at 1-877-980-4450.

Printed in the United States of America

Find us on

Contents

Libya is a country in Africa. People have lived there for thousands of years. In the past, different groups, such as the Romans, ruled what's now Libya. Today, it's an independent country.

Many people live in Libya today. They come from different parts of the world.

Over 6 million people live there.

Libyans have many different jobs. Some work in schools or hospitals. Others work in oil fields or on construction sites. Factory workers in Libya make products including **textiles** and **chemicals**. Farmers grow fruits and grains.

Libya has many stunning places to visit. The country is home to mountains and huge deserts. The country also has beautiful

Misrata, Libya's third-largest city, is home to lovely beaches and a busy trading center.

beaches. **Ruins** from the past are seen by visitors from around the world.

The culture, or way of life, of Libya is unique—unlike any other culture. Libyans enjoy music and the arts. They also like playing sports such as soccer and volleyball. Every year, festivals and celebrations take place throughout the country. Libya is an exciting place to explore!

Libya is in North Africa. Above it lies the Mediterranean Sea. Countries bordering Libya are Algeria, Tunisia, Niger, Chad, Sudan, and Egypt.

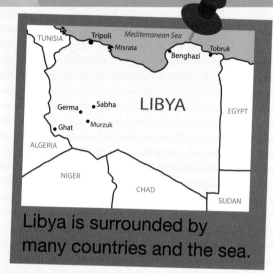

Libya is surrounded by many countries and the sea.

Libya covers 679,362 square miles (1,759,540 square kilometers). The country is slightly larger than the state of Alaska.

Libya has different land features. Coastal plains run along Libya's shoreline. Most of the nation's population lives here. Close to the coastal plains

FACT!

Libya's highest point is called Bikku Bitti.

are mountains. Examples include the Akhdar Mountains in the east and the Nafusah Mountains in the west. Libya also has lots of deserts. The Sahara is the most well known

Sand dunes in Libya's deserts shift with the winds.

desert in the world, and part of it is in Libya.

Libya has no rivers. Instead, it has **wadis** that fill with water when it rains.

Most of Libya has a hot and dry climate, or weather. However, the coastal lowlands have mild winters and warm summers.

Great Man-Made River

The Great Man-Made River is a pipeline network that brings water from under the Sahara to cities on Libya's coast.

History

Libya has existed for thousands of years. In ancient times, different groups, like the Phoenicians, Greeks, and Romans, ruled parts of Libya.

Arab armies arrived in the seventh century CE. Many people started to believe in Islam. During the early 1500s, a group called the Ottoman Empire controlled Libya. They ruled until 1911, when Italy took over. Libya belonged to Italy until 1945, when World War II ended.

The ancient city Leptis Magna has many Roman ruins.

FACT!

Descendants of the first people in Libya are called Berbers.

King Idris

King Idris was the first leader of independent Libya. He served from 1951 to 1969.

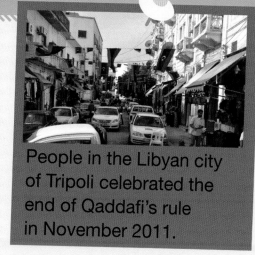

People in the Libyan city of Tripoli celebrated the end of Qaddafi's rule in November 2011.

Libya became an independent country in 1951. Eight years later, oil was discovered. Oil brought lots of money to Libya.

Army officers overthrew Libya's king in 1969. Then, Muammar al-Qaddafi became a leader called a **dictator**. He fought with many nations and made deals with bad people called terrorists.

Libyans fought against Qaddafi's rule. He was killed in 2011. In 2012, the country held its first democratic elections in over 40 years. However, Libya still faces many challenges today.

VOTE

Libya has 22 sections, called districts. These districts are like states. The nation's capital city is Tripoli.

Shown here are people at a meeting of Libya's House of Representatives.

Libya's government has been changing since the death of Qaddafi in 2011. Different groups have been fighting to control the country. In 2015, some of the groups came together and agreed to form the Government of National Accord (GNA). Most other countries see it as the true government of Libya.

All Libyan citizens over the age of 18 may vote in elections.

Women in Government

Libya's House of Representatives has 200 members. At least 32 of them must be women. Each of the 102 city councils also must have at least one female member.

People go through a security check before voting in Benghazi, Libya.

The GNA is led by a group called the Presidential Council. The House of Representatives, which writes new laws, is also part of the GNA, but it doesn't back the Presidential Council.

A new version of the country's laws, called a constitution, was written in 2017. It has not yet been fully put in place. Libyans hope to hold new elections soon. They want to choose leaders to take over for the GNA, which isn't meant to last forever.

The Economy

Most of Libya's money comes from oil or gas. Libya trades these things with countries around the world. Its trading partners include Italy, China, Turkey, and Spain. The

Students head to their classrooms at an elementary school in Benghazi.

country's money is the Libyan dinar.

About six out of ten Libyan workers have service jobs. Some work for oil companies or banks. Others have jobs in hotels, restaurants, and health care. The education field also employs people in

Libya produces about 1.1 million barrels of oil every day!

Some people in Libya make and sell crafts, like leather goods, rugs, silver jewelry, and glassware.

Colorful rugs are just some of the items for sale at a Libyan market.

Libya, which means it gives them jobs.

Libyan factory workers make different kinds of products, including steel. Libya also makes chemicals and food products such as olive oil. Tripoli and Benghazi are two important manufacturing cities.

Fewer than 20 percent of Libyans work in farming. The country gets most of its food from other countries. That's because deserts take up so much of Libya's land. It's hard to grow food in a desert.

The Environment

Libya is home to many animals and plants. Rodents like the jerboa live in desert areas. Hyenas, foxes, and gazelles live there too. Hawks, eagles, and vultures are common

This fennec fox is sleeping in the sand.

birds in Libya. Adders and kraits are two types of poisonous snakes that live in Libya. They can be found around water holes or **oases**.

FACT!

The fennec fox is the world's smallest fox, and it can be found in Libya. Its big ears help it keep cool in the Sahara heat.

All of Libya's electricity comes from fossil fuels like oil and gas. **Renewable energy**, like solar power, could also be used in the future.

Forests are found in the Akhdar Mountains. Many kinds of grasses also grow in Libya. Few plants can survive in Libya's deserts, but date palms grow well in oases.

This man is sitting in the sand at an oasis in Libya.

Water pollution is a big problem along Libya's coast. There's also a lack of fresh water for people.

Dry, hot winds known as *ghibli* happen in spring and fall. They cause dangerous, or unsafe, sandstorms and dust storms.

Libya is home to different **ethnic groups**. Berber and Arab people make up about 97 percent of the population. Most Berber people in Libya have adopted the Arab culture, but not all.

Shown here is a Libyan family walking on the streets of Tripoli.

About 3 percent of people in Libya belong to other ethnic groups. People of Greek, Maltese, and Italian backgrounds

The average person in Libya lives to be 76 or 77 years old.

The Tuareg

The Tuareg people are herders in the Sahara. That means they move, or herd, animals like sheep or goats across the desert. They have their own language and customs, or ways of acting. They live in southern Libya, but they also travel throughout North Africa.

This group of Tuareg men lead their camels through the Sahara.

often live in **urban** areas. There are also groups from South Asia and the Middle East. Some of the nation's workers come from other parts of northern Africa. They call Libya their home too.

About four out of five Libyan people live in towns or cities. Libya's largest city is Tripoli. It has over 1.1 million people. Most families in Libyan cities live in apartments. Wealthier

The skyline of Tripoli shows apartment buildings of all shapes and sizes.

people may live in large homes. Some people have their own cars. Others travel by bus or taxi.

It's more common for Libyans in farming areas to live in houses. Homes are often built out of bricks that have dried in the sun. In the Sahara,

Most Libyan families have two children.

Women in the Workforce

Around 25 percent of Libya's workforce is female. The most common jobs for women are doctors and teachers. Some Libyan women also start businesses. Examples include sewing or baking businesses. These jobs are done at home.

some houses are even built underground! Roads in the Libyan countryside are often unpaved.

Internet use is becoming more popular in Libya. Cell phones are common too.

Covered passageways in Libya help keep people cool in the blazing desert heat.

Religion

Islam is the official religion, or belief system, of Libya. More than 96 percent of Libyans are Muslim. Nearly all of them follow the Sunni branch of Islam.

Muslims celebrate Eid al-Fitr in Libya by praying in Martyrs' Square in Tripoli.

Muslims pray five times a day. The holy day of the week is Friday. Men go to a holy building, called a mosque, to pray. Women usually pray at

FACT!

In 2018, Libya opened Imam Al-Bukhari Mosque in Tripoli. It is the country's largest mosque and can hold up to 2,400 people.

Eating Food

Muslims can't eat certain foods. These foods include all pork products.

home. There are many religious holidays in Libya. Eid al-Fitr is a three-day celebration that follows the holy month of Ramadan. People visit friends and family to pray and eat together.

The second most practiced religion in Libya is Christianity. Almost 3 percent of people follow it. Libya also has small groups of Buddhists and Hindus.

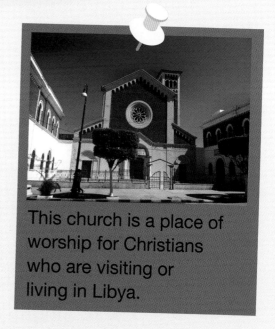

This church is a place of worship for Christians who are visiting or living in Libya.

Language

Arabic is the official language of Libya. Nearly everyone in the country speaks it. Libyans speak a kind of Arabic called Libyan Arabic. However, official documents and

Friends in Libya enjoy talking together.

schools use Modern Standard Arabic. This type of Arabic is used all over the Arab world.

Lots of Libyans speak more than one language. Berbers often speak Arabic and Nafusi.

FACT!

About 30,000 people in Libya speak Domari. It's an Indo-European language, meaning it's connected to languages from Europe and Asia.

Script

Arabic letters are connected in a script rather than separated like English print letters. It can be written with beautiful **calligraphy**.

The Tuareg frequently speak Tamashek and Arabic. English is the most common second language in Libya. It's often used for government and business. Italian and French are other popular second languages. Immigrants, or people who move from one country to a new country, often speak their home country's languages.

Many road signs in Libya are written in different languages.

Arts and Festivals

People in Libya create and enjoy art. Weaving and sewing are popular. Metal engravings, or drawings in metal, are another kind of Libyan art. Like Muslims around the world, Libyan artists do not show animals or people in their art. Instead, their artworks include patterns and writing.

The colorful tiles at Gurgi Mosque in Tripoli show typical Islamic designs.

Both dancing and music are popular in

Graffiti, or painting on buildings and in public places without permission, has become a popular art form in the 21st century.

Rock Art

Tadrart Acacus is a famous historical site in Libya. Its caves have thousands of paintings. Some date back to 12,000 BCE!

Libya. Each part of the country has its own folk dances. Libyan musicians play many instruments. The *zokra* is like bagpipes. The *darbuka* is a type of drum.

This group of Libyan girls performs a celebration dance in Tripoli in 2015.

Some musicians also play music that combines Libyan music with European pop music.

Independence Day is on December 24. This national holiday marks when Libya declared independence in 1951. People wave flags and celebrate in cities around the country.

There are many ways to have fun in Libya. People watch or play sports, share stories, or enjoy games with friends and family.

This photo shows members of Libya's national soccer team.

Soccer is the country's most popular sport. All people can play soccer, though many Libyan families don't like girls playing sports. Libya has several soccer teams. Some Libyans also enjoy basketball, volleyball, and tennis. Water

FACT!

Libyan athletes won 60 medals at the 2019 Special Olympics World Games.

sports are becoming more popular.

Libyans spend time with friends too. Men often meet friends at cafés and play games like chess or cards. Women shop with friends or visit friends at their homes.

Female friends often talk and laugh together at home after having tea.

Families often watch movies at home in Libya. Younger people also enjoy playing video games. Board games are popular too. *Zamma* is a popular board game similar to checkers.

Racing in Libya

Horse racing is exciting and enjoyed by many in Libya. Car racing is also quite popular throughout the country.

Food

People in Libya enjoy many different types of food. They like to eat lots of fresh vegetables and fruits. Libyans often eat potatoes, onions, and peas. Popular fruits include dates, watermelon, and grapes. Many dishes are served with couscous, a small, beaded pasta. Some say that couscous is the country's national dish.

Couscous, in the center of this plate, is served with vegetables, lamb, and chicken.

In desert areas, Tuareg people bake bread using the hot sand as an oven.

Magrud

Magrud is the name of a well-loved Libyan dessert. This cookie is stuffed with dates, then soaked in a honey syrup. It's perfect for people with a sweet tooth!

Magrud can be served alongside sweet green tea and mint.

Shorba libiya is a traditional Libyan dish. It's a soup made of tomato and lamb broth, chickpeas, orzo pasta, herbs, and spices. The most popular meat in Libya is lamb. It's used in stews and many other dishes.

People in Libya often drink coffee and tea. The tea is usually sweet and served with mint.

Glossary

calligraphy Decorative lettering or handwriting.

chemical Matter that can be mixed with other matter to cause changes.

descendant Someone related to a person or group of people who lived at an earlier time.

dictator A person who rules with total authority, often in a cruel manner.

ethnic group People who share a common culture or ancestry.

oasis A spot in the desert that has trees, grass, and water.

renewable energy Power that comes from things in nature that can be used over and over again, such as sunlight, wind, and water.

ruin A part of an anicent building that is still standing.

textile A type of woven cloth or fabric.

urban Related to a city or a town.

wadi A valley or channel that is dry except during the rainy season.

Find Out More

Books

Falola, Toyin, Jason Morgan, and Bukola A. Oyeniyi. *Culture and Customs of Libya*. Santa Barbara, CA: Greenwood, 2012.

O'Neal, Claire. *We Visit Libya*. Hockessin, DE: Mitchell Lane Publishers, 2013.

Website

Britannica Kids: Libya

kids.britannica.com/kids/article/Libya/345728

This site offers information about Libya, as well as photos from all over the country.

Video

Unseen Sahara: Libya from the Sky

www.youtube.com/watch?v=6f4TC7qZl9g

This wordless video from *National Geographic* shows the Libyan desert from above, as a photographer traveled over in a paraglider.

Index

About the Author

Alicia Z. Klepeis began her career at the National Geographic Society. She is the author of over 100 kids' books, including *How Smartphones Work*, *The World's Strangest Foods*, and *Francisco's Kites*. She would love to see the oases, deserts, and coastal cities in Libya.